OUTSIDE THE BOX

WORKBOOK

Cover design by Sara Young

ISBN: 978-1-959095-88-0   1 2 3 4 5 6 7 8 9 10

Printed in the United States of America

DR. BARTHOLOMEW ORR

OUTSIDE THE BOX

INNOVATIVE CHANGE FOR MORE EFFECTIVE MINISTRY

WORKBOOK

CONTENTS

OUTSIDE THE BOX
WORKBOOK

Observing the detrimental influence of our culture on our families, communities, and nation, Dr. Orr offers insights into how the church will once again become a powerful change agent in our society. He describes profound truths for individual leaders and for entire churches that will guide the trajectory of their lives as they seek to build God's Kingdom. Within these pages, Dr. Orr reveals the profound significance and impact of our Message, Maturity, Mentoring, Missions, and Ministry, as well as how to Multiply our impact, why we should collectively Marvel at God's work, and how to achieve Monumental Innovation at this juncture in history.

As our world continues to change, the church must stay ahead of the curve and strategically lead in our communities, while steadfastly holding on to foundational truths. Join Dr. Orr as he unfolds how our current and future impact requires us to think and act *Outside the Box*.

FOUNDATIONS OF CHANGE

CHAPTER 1

MESSAGE: BATTLING FAKE NEWS

"As was Paul's custom, he went to the synagogue service, and for three Sabbaths in a row he used the scriptures to reason with the people. He explained the prophecies and proved that the Messiah must suffer and rise from the dead. He said, 'This Jesus I'm telling you about is the Messiah.'"
Acts 17:2-3 (NLT)

If you were to hear the phrase "Trustworthy professions," which ones would first come to mind? On the other hand, if you heard "Untrustworthy professions," which fields of work would hit the top of your list? Trust is easily lost and usually requires time to build. In our society, and around the world, it's gotten so bad that people don't know what to believe or who they can truly trust to speak the truth. Fake News abounds—misinformation, disinformation, outright lies, and "my personal truth." This situation is not new to our 21st century; it's been around a whole lot longer than our lifetimes. Fake News surrounded Jesus Christ. The religious leaders of His day would not have been able to have Him crucified if it weren't for Fake News. Let me show you what I'm talking about.

Matthew 26:59-61 (NLT) states:

"The leading priests and the entire high council were trying to find witnesses who would lie about Jesus, so they could put him to death. But even though they found many who agreed to give a false witness, they could not use anyone's testimony. Finally, two men came forward who declared, 'This Man said, "I am able to destroy the Temple of God and rebuild it in three days."'"

After He was crucified and was buried in the grave, He rose the third day early in the morning. Pay attention to the guards when you read this account. An earthquake shook the place and the guards witnessed everything. Look what happened in Matthew 28:11-15 (NLT):

"As the women were on their way, some of the guards went into the city and told the leading priests what had happened. A meeting with the elders was called, and they decided to give the soldiers a large bribe. They told the soldiers, 'You must say, "Jesus' disciples came during the

night while we were sleeping, and they stole His body." If the governor hears about it, we'll stand up for you so you won't get in trouble.' So the guards accepted the bribe and said what they were told to say. Their story spread widely among the Jews, and they still tell it today."

Fake News! The guards told the religious leaders, "The ground started shaking. That stone rolled away. There were angels!" But that was not the narrative the council wanted to be known. "No, we can't tell that one! But here's the story we want you to tell." And they're still telling it! Oh, Fake News! Even in Acts 17 when Paul and Silas were in Thessalonica, we see them being affected by Fake News! They were spreading the message of Jesus Christ and were hit with misleading information that caused a great disturbance in the entire city, forcing them to leave.

What are some examples of Fake News that you have heard about God, His people, or His church?

_____

_____

_____

_____

_____

_____

_____

_____

We are in a battle to declare and defend the truths we read in the Bible. It is up to each one of us to know the message of Jesus Christ and exemplify it to our individual spheres of influence. We all are responsible to fight against Fake News! Unfortunately, much has been said and done by Christians that make people hesitant to truth the church. We have much to undo.

Why do you think the church has lost the influence in our culture that it once had?

_____

_____

_____

_____

_____

_____

_____

We as leaders and as entire churches must reignite our passion for God's true Word and to make it known to others. Let us push forward the Gospel of Jesus with clarity and consistency to produce powerful change in our churches and communities. Becoming well-established in certain biblical truths will lead to such impact!

DECLARING TRUTH

Each Christian must be clear about what God says concerning *redemption*. This word means the act of being saved from something; to regain possession of something in exchange for payment, or payment of a debt. I call this *the salvation Jesus brings.*

Read Romans 1:16. What does the Apostle Paul describe as the power of God for salvation?

_____

_____

_____

_____

_____

_____

He is going back to the cross of Jesus Christ. He is letting his listeners know that Jesus Christ died on a cross, but it was necessary for Him to die to redeem, or purchase back, our sinful souls from eternal condemnation. As we consider the cross and Jesus' death on it, it is vital to understand it well enough ourselves so that we can clearly communicate it to others.

What are some keywords or phrases that come to mind when thinking about the Gospel of Jesus Christ? Consider words that you would use when sharing the Good News with someone.

_____

_____

_____

_____

_____

_____

Now take 60 seconds to verbally state the Gospel as clearly and concisely as you can, using these keywords as a guide.

_____

_____

_____

_____

_____

_____

_____

If we are going to be saved, washed of our sins, forgiven for the wrongs we've done, the only way is through the cross of Jesus Christ. This message is our bedrock and must be the foundation of every Christian ministry, inside the church walls and outside them.

Read the following verses and then write a summary of them in your own words—Acts 4:12, John 14:6

_____

_____

_____

_____

_____

_____

_____

_____

_____

These truths are a bedrock and are non-negotiable to our faith in Jesus Christ. Yet you likely have heard people's opinions about what it takes to go to Heaven—in other words, the Fake News about salvation. What are some Fake News ideas that you have heard about salvation?

_____

_____

_____

_____

_____

_____

_____

_____

_____

_____

_____

_____

Salvation is not in Buddha. Salvation is not in Muhammad. Salvation is not in Eastern meditation or positive thinking. Salvation is only found in Jesus Christ. People can be sincere about their beliefs . . . and sincerely wrong. But each follower of Christ must be firm on these important truths from scripture so that we will "*. . . no longer be immature like children. We won't be tossed and blown about by every wind of new teaching. We will not be influenced when people try to trick us with lies so clever, they sound like the truth*" (Ephesians 4:14-15, NLT). Doing our biblical homework will prepare us for when we face a test in conversations about spiritual matters!

Let's also get clear about **righteousness**. I call this *the standard Jesus demands*. This consists of the lifestyle that ought to depict someone who follows Christ.

Read 1 Thessalonians 1:6-7. How is the church at Thessalonica described by Paul?

_____

_____

_____

_____

_____

_____

_____

_____

_____

This is the standard Jesus demands. You see, when we get saved Jesus is expecting each one of us to live a sanctified, holy, righteous life. He is calling us not to blend in with the world or to live like the world, but to live a holy, set-apart life. All of us ought to have a testimony like that.

We all have sinned and fallen short of God's perfection and glory—we're all guilty sinners before God. But, because of God's amazing kindness and grace, *"if any man be in Christ, he is a new creature; old things are passed away; behold, all things are become new"* (2 Corinthians 5:17, KJV). One powerful word that describes a forgiven sinner is "justified," or declared innocent before God. This means that there is no longer judgment for those sins. This is just one of many characteristics of followers of Christ.

Take a few moments to read Ephesians 1:3-14 to better grasp what an amazing work of salvation was performed by God in His forgiven children. Then write down what you observe.

_____

_____

_____

_____

_____

_____

_____

_____

I'm sure you can envision the wonderful changes in your family, church, and community if living a holy, God-honoring lifestyle became the great treasure of our hearts. *"Be holy, because I am holy,"* God commands His people (1 Peter 1:16, BSB). Do you think your world would look different if this became a foundational expectation among Christ-followers? We must not only know the truth about redemption and righteousness, but we also need all believers to live out the truth. Let's live out the truth, putting it into practice, humbly and consistently—in the home, in the church, in the office, on Sundays, and on Friday nights.

Furthermore, look at God's charge regarding our **responsibility**. I call this *the sharing Jesus commanded*. What is the responsibility of followers of Jesus Christ when it comes to the message of the cross?

Read the following verses and then write what calling is given to Christians: 2 Corinthians 5:20; Acts 1:8.

_____

_____

_____

_____

_____

_____

_____

Why do you think the vast majority of Christians do not align themselves with this calling?

_____

_____

_____

_____

_____

We preach to persuade. We teach to persuade. We witness to persuade. We're trying to win as many souls as possible to Jesus Christ. When you do speak of God, is your message simply to share biographical information about Him? Is it crafted to convince people of their need for a Savior? Are you trying to persuade others to follow Jesus, and help others to do the same?

I'm sure you've heard the phrase, "Where God guides, He provides." It's true. Since He has given us a calling to share about Him with those near and far, He has graciously given us His Spirit. *"But you will receive power when the Holy Spirit comes upon you. And you will be my witnesses ,telling people about me everywhere — in Jerusalem, throughout Judea, in Samaria, and to the ends of the earth"* (Acts 1:8, NLT).

Our message needs the guidance and power of the Holy Spirit. Invite Him in prayer to lead you before you speak to someone. Ask Him for opportunities to share about Him, courage to open your mouth, and wisdom to know what to say. And this is why reading and studying scripture is so vital—the more Truth you learn, the more that the Holy Spirit can bring to your mind in different situations you will face. It can be likened to one wise warrior who fills his quiver with countless arrows vs. a foolish one who takes only a few. The former will be victorious due to greater preparation. Approach your battles prepared—feast on the Word and commit to reading it every day.

To wrap up this chapter, let's consider one more series of observations about how Paul communicated the message of Christ at Thessalonica. Read Acts 17:2-3.

Paul exemplifies four strategies that, I believe, are also meant for each one of us. First, he *reasoned with them*. For three Sabbath days, he went into the synagogue with a plan to discuss parts of the Old Testament with his Jewish listeners. "Reason" means to dialogue. It means to question and to answer.

What are some questions you can ask others to possibly open a door to a discussion on spiritual matters?

_____

_____

_____

_____

_____

Some seasoned communicators and evangelists will approach this topic by asking seekers: "What is your purpose in life? What hope sustains you in challenging times? What are your beliefs about Jesus? What happens after death? How did you arrive at your beliefs about spiritual matters?" Not only should you actively listen but be ready to share thoughtful answers to these questions from your experience!

Next, Paul *explained to them*. He explained the prophecies of the coming Messiah to them. He "fully opened" the scriptures, which is what "explained" means. There are vast resources in church libraries and online that demonstrate how perfectly Jesus and His life met the myriad of prophecies hundreds of years before His birth. The mathematical probability is minuscule that anyone would even be able to meet a handful of those predictions. Jesus met them all! Knowing these would be helpful in your explanations to others.

Thirdly, he *proved it*. The word "prove" means that he laid the biblical evidence "close beside or next to" the facts to justify his claims about Jesus. Some individuals seek proof. While many will debate various topics you lay before them, one thing no one can deny is your own testimony of how Jesus saved and changed you. This is your story

. . . amidst His Story! Tie in what He has done and is doing in you. The world wants to know if your faith holds any power, so humbly put on display the wonder-working God you know personally! Then lead them to confront the reality with a response.

Fourth, we see that Paul was intent to *proclaim it*. Say it, write it, announce it, tweet it, DM it, post it, share it however we can. I challenge you to make Him known in one way today to someone else. Then come back and share your story with another! Be unique. Be strategic. Be creative in your message. But don't keep it to yourself, Friend! Let your faith go viral. Why not leave an impact and let the world know about Jesus Christ?

An integral foundation of change is getting the Message of Jesus right! It involves knowing the truth, living out the truth, and speaking the truth with conviction, urgency, and compassion. The truth is found in the Bible and doesn't need to be sugarcoated or watered down. Like Paul and Jesus, we need not strive to be politically correct. The essential foundation is that we, and those we lead, must hold firmly to this cornerstone truth—there is salvation in no other person and no other thing apart from Jesus Christ.

GOING DEEPER

1. What are some key components of the Gospel message?

_____

_____

_____

_____

_____

_____

2. Describe the standards that God expects of His followers.

_____

_____

_____

_____

_____

_____

_____

3. Name two strategies to communicate Jesus more effectively to others.

_____

_____

_____

_____

_____

_____

CHAPTER 2

MATURITY: GROWING DEEPER & GOING HIGHER

"So we tell others about Christ, warning everyone and teaching everyone with all the wisdom God has given us. We want to present them to God, perfect in their relationship to Christ. That's why I work and struggle so hard, depending on Christ's mighty power that works within me."
—Colossians 1:28-29 (NLT)

Our times cry out for maturity! It is given that physical bodies gradually mature; emotional stability will naturally occur; intellectual abilities will mature. But there is no assurance that a person will spiritually mature. We see the fruits of spiritual deadness all around us among those who do not follow Jesus. Apart from faith in Jesus Christ, we are all separated from God and walk in darkness (Ephesians 5:8). The sinfulness of the world doesn't come as a surprise, does it? What is saddening and surprising, though, is the immaturity among those who made a commitment to follow Jesus. From this we observe compromise among Christians, corruption among clergy, and conflict within our churches.

What are some signs of spiritual immaturity? What effect could this have on others?

_____

_____

_____

_____

_____

Since maturity is not automatic with age, association, achievement, or announcement, we must all work to grow up! There are some 20+, 30+, 40+ year-olds that are still childish and immature. Even within the church you have people that have been saved 20, 30, or 40 years who are still undisciplined, unruly, and unkind. Similarly, maturity is not automatic with association. Just attending a church for months or even decades doesn't ensure that someone will know Christ more intimately or will demonstrate a lifestyle that mirrors His character. It isn't achieved through worldly success either. We all know people in high-profile roles who need an intense course on how to mature—not just spiritually but in all areas of life. Lastly, maturity doesn't come when someone announces that he or she has arrived at the peak of Mount Maturity. One's life will clearly display who is and who is not mature, regardless of their verbal declaration.

On the contrary, what are signs that a person *is demonstrating* spiritual maturity?

_____

_____

_____

_____

_____

_____

_____

One demonstration of maturity involves actively pursuing unity among Christ's followers. Read John 17:22-23. What did Jesus pray for those who would follow Him?

_____

_____

_____

_____

_____

Read Acts 4:42-47. What regular practices took place that strengthened unity among first-century Christians? What message do you think spoke to the community around them?

_____

_____

_____

_____

_____

_____

_____

_____

There is a greater purpose to our unity than simply being nice to each other. Unity among Christians proclaims a message about Jesus and His ability to unite people of varying preferences, backgrounds, and affiliations. When there is spiritual maturity, there is holy cooperation, unity, and working side-by-side for the glory of God. This powerful expression of God's presence serves as a foundation for change personally and in our communities, and we must daily choose to make it a reality. Therefore, how do we develop spiritually and help others mature as well?

This aim must be the goal of every Christian leader—to guide, strengthen, and encourage all believers in Christ to become more like Him. Do your interactions with other Christians matter? Absolutely! Paul writes to the Colossian Christians about this exact point.

Look again at Colossians 1:28-29. What was Paul's goal? What did he do regularly to bring it to fulfillment?

_____

_____

_____

_____

_____

_____

_____

_____

The challenge with the church at Colosse is the same challenge we face today—how do we *"present them to God, perfect in their relationship to Christ"*? In that day and time, false teaching had gotten into the church and was leading some in the church away from biblical truths. The same thing is happening now. People inside and outside the church are being misled by ear-tingling beliefs, some of which are so subtly deceptive. Maturing in our faith builds a strong foundation of truth that enables us to recognize and defend against those errors.

To do so, you have got to **work in the Word**. If we hope to have a maturing faith in Jesus, we must take definite steps to get scripture into us, internalizing and implementing the wisdom of God. I call this *the study of God's Word*. We cannot be spiritually mature if we don't know the Word of God. If any of us are going to grow, there must be consistency in this essential discipline! How often do you get into the Word of God? How much of it are you allowing to *get into you*? We need to make sure that we are "rightly dividing" the word of truth (2 Timothy 2:15) and studying the Bible.

The psalmist got it right when he wrote, *"How can a young man keep his way pure? By guarding it according to Your word. With all my heart I have sought You; do not let me stray from Your commandments. I have hidden Your word in my heart that I might not sin against You."* (Psalm 119:9-11, BSB).

How else does the Word of God help us?

_____

_____

_____

_____

_____

_____

_____

_____

_____

From scripture, we learn God's Word, seek to understand it with its instructions and promises, and hold to it in every season of life, good or bad, until we reach Glory! It is useful for teaching, correcting, rebuking, and training us to be righteous and holy. Every single believer and every church needs a deeper understanding of God's Word. Without it, we cannot mature. As Paul described in Ephesians 6:17 (NLT), take *"the sword of the Spirit, which is the Word of God."*

Why do you believe Paul described it as a sword?

_____

_____

_____

_____

_____

_____

_____

_____

_____

In turn, we then impress these wonderful instructions and promises on others. As Jesus explained, we plant and water. This is our responsibility. Where the seed grows is not under our control. If you spoke that word of truth out of love and in humility, release your grasp and let the Lord work in His time to grow those seeds. I find solace in remembering what Paul wrote: *"I planted the seed, Apollos watered it, but God has been making it grow"* (1 Corinthians 3:6, NIV). Leave your acts of obedience in others' hearts and minds for the Lord to develop.

In baking, you mix ingredients into a lump of dough until you cannot separate one ingredient from another. It all mixes thoroughly. In the same way, the Word is intentionally intermingled into our minds and spirits as we continue adding other scriptures, sermons, and biblical truths. With these seeds of truth, the Holy Spirit will draw from and bring them to mind at the proper time for ourselves or for another. The more of God's Word there is in us to pull from, the more useful we can be to share with others. Without a storage of God's Word in us, there is little to offer others in the way of biblical instruction, encouragement, and hope. A regular diet of scriptural truths will strengthen our faith, produce confidence, instill direction, and yield hope.

There is no power for true change apart from His truth, and all of God's people need to know this is a reality for you. What is your plan to put more of God's Word in you?

_____

_____

_____

_____

_____

_____

_____

_____

_____

Not only do we feed on God's truths from the Bible, but we must obey them. Jesus said, *"If you love Me, obey my commandments"* (John 14:15, NLT). We all have experienced those people who say a whole lot of scripture but do not live it out. You've met them, I'm sure! What a turn-off to not just Christians, but especially to non-Christians, along with the residual harm it produces. Following God is to follow His instructions. **Maturity comes not just by hearing the truth, but by obeying it.**

That involves meeting together regularly with other followers of Christ. Read Hebrews 10:25. What is the author instructing and how would that affect spiritual maturity?

_____

_____

_____

_____

_____

_____

_____

_____

This is why we come to church and spend time with God's people. We approach this table to get a balanced diet of listening to biblical preachers, Kingdom-focused music, and godly people! Sadly, many Christians choose to avoid this spiritual buffet out of apathy, sin, or distraction. I once heard a pastor say to his congregation, "Show me your friends and I'll show you your future." That which we input will sooner or later become our output. A man reaps what he sows. Community is a gift that God gave us, and we all need it to stay nearer to Him and to become all He called us to be. **In short, being in the presence of God, His Word, and His people will have a profound effect on a life, yielding more mature fruit than those without these essential influences.**

Our calling involves not only working *in* the Word (reading it, studying it, memorizing it, meditating on it, and rightly dividing it daily) but also a second component of deepening our maturity: *working out the wrinkles*. I call this *the struggles of our flesh*. Every person consists of previous experiences, influences, education, trauma, family, and culture. Is all of that going to be godly? No! All of us need God to undo and re-do our thinking, motivations, and behaviors.

Read Romans 12:1-2 and explain what needs to be done to understand God's will.

_____

_____

_____

_____

_____

_____

_____

For Christians, some behaviors must be completely cut out of our lives. They do not belong any longer! Read Colossians 3:5-9. Name some qualities and actions that must be fully discarded.

_____

_____

_____

_____

_____

_____

_____

Offering your body as a living sacrifice? Renewing your mind? "What did I sign up for, God?" Rest assured! I can tell you that everything God asks us to lay down, He fills up more with Himself and with a joy that surpasses any pleasure of the world.

If a Christian or a church family is going to mature spiritually, there must be the continual yielding of their lives to be transformed into the image of Jesus Christ. There is no easy way around it. Being a disciple of Jesus is a call to surrender, to live for Him above all other affections until the day we take our final breath. Jesus exemplified the right mindset of yielding to the Father when He prayed in the garden, *"Yet not My will, but Yours be done"* (Luke 22:42, BSB).

May God form in us a spirit of surrender and a spirit of holiness. No matter what we were or what we used to do, we ought to be working out the wrinkles in our lives, so His character is more clearly seen through us. As John the Baptist confessed, *"He must increase; I must decrease"* (John 3:30, BSB).

What areas of your life do you see that need to be undone or redone? How willing are you to yield in those areas?

_____

_____

_____

_____

_____

_____

We need the Holy Spirit to empower this change. There is a changing of heart that only God's Spirit can initiate and work out in us. He also equips us to accomplish other Christian responsibilities, like loving others unconditionally. Paul reminds his young mentee, Timothy, about what else has changed: *"For the Spirit God gave us does not make us timid, but gives us power, love and self-discipline"* (2 Timothy 1:7).

Do you lack the strength, the willpower, the self-control to obey Him in some areas? Well, you've got the supernatural power of God inside you through that yielded position of your heart, empowering you to do what is too difficult to do on your own. *"Be strong in the Lord and in the strength of His might"* (Ephesians 6:10, NASB). The Holy Spirit is the true source of empowerment to become like Jesus, and we mustn't rush past Him in our busyness because we think that we've got it covered. We don't. We need Him.

In essence, what God is saying is, "Let Me help you work out the wrinkles." Whatever the issues or the habits that you have, allow the Word and My Spirit to make changes inside you. To work out the wrinkles, you need God's Word and God's Spirit! Today, have you yielded to the Holy Spirit and invited Him to work His power in you? Write out a prayer of yielding and confession to God.

_____

_____

_____

_____

_____

_____

The only question is if we will plug into that supernatural power instead of relying on our own efforts to do what is right.

If we are going to be mature, we need to **work up a win**! I call this *the signs of our faith*. How do we work up a win? What does that life look like? It's not just a good life He seeks; it's a godly and fruitful life. A fruitful life consists of the deeds that we do, the attitudes we convey, the words we speak. In other words, God is expecting us to treat people with compassion, fairness, and goodness. He expects us to serve one another, to honor others, to do good for them as we have opportunity.

Paul gets very practical with his readers in Colossians 3:12-15. Read this passage slowly and name three of these actions that would make an impact on families and communities.

_____

_____

_____

_____

_____

_____

If you want to live a fruitful life, it will be marked by good deeds. Don't do it for pats on the back. Don't do it for your name to be called out by the pastor. Do it to point others to Jesus Christ! Bringing glory to Him is the primary goal and should be the motivation for any goodness that flows from you.

Get into the habit of praying, "Search me, Lord . . . If you find anything that shouldn't be here, enable me to lay it down and cling to You instead." It's time to stop playing games. Growing up is a foundation of change in our homes, churches, and communities. Without it, we lose all credibility. Strive to live as a holy saint! Look more like Jesus! Love one another! Grow up in your living! Grow up in your giving! This world needs mature disciples and our churches need maturing disciples to lead others to do the same.

As physical maturity is a long, slow process, so it is with spiritual maturity. Be patient with yourself and with others. Trust in God's abundant grace when you fail, and rely on His grace to get back up and keep walking in obedience. The enemy would have you weighed down in despair and discouragement, but your loving Father calls out to you to stand up and walk toward Him yet again.

Maturity is only going to start when we work in the Word, work out the wrinkles, and work up a win, all of which bring glory to Him.

GOING DEEPER

1. What is the Lord calling you to lay down in surrender and to pick up as a godly habit?

_____

_____

_____

_____

_____

_____

2. Is it your responsibility to make the faith of others grow? What part of discipleship is your responsibility?

_____

_____

_____

_____

_____

_____

3. What steps can you take to invest God's Word into others?

_____

_____

_____

_____

_____

_____

FORWARDING THE CHANGE

CHAPTER 3

MENTORING: BREAKING & CREATING CYCLES

"Timothy, my dear son, be strong through the grace that God gives you in Christ Jesus. You have heard me teach things that have been confirmed by many reliable witnesses. Now teach these truths to other trustworthy people who will be able to pass them on to others."
—2 Timothy 2:1-2 (NLT)

I don't believe in generational curses, but I do believe in generational cycles. I do believe the reality that some bad habits keep getting repeated. Haven't you seen some negative habits or cycles in your own family, or those in your church? Perhaps it's the cycle of teenage pregnancy or pregnancy outside of marriage. Maybe it is the cycle of deadbeat dads, absent fathers, drug addiction, gambling, or pornography. There are cycles of drug abuse, sexual promiscuity, homosexuality, lesbianism, poverty, ignorance, and inferiority complexes. I do believe that these cycles are sometimes repeated among families from generation to generation.

What negative habits or cycles have you observed in your own family or circle of friends?

_____

_____

_____

_____

_____

_____

Why do we allow ungodly cycles to repeat and what can be done about them? Moreover, what is God's will for His people as it relates to building His Kingdom here on earth? To fulfill His purposes for us individually and as a church, we must intentionally and strategically forward on the change that He has graciously worked inside us. **If we don't pass it on, then healing stops with us . . . Freedom stops with us . . . Victory stops with us.**

One of God's answers to this dilemma is a life-on-life investment called "Mentoring"—investing in the lives of those in our sphere of influence: other pastors and leaders, those within our own families, those at church, at work, or in the neighborhood. The goal is simple: help someone else to increasingly love and obey Jesus, while helping him or her to become a better leader. Methods may differ, and a host of topics can be discussed, but the goal is the same—to increasingly follow Jesus in every area of life.

Have you ever been mentored? Have you ever mentored someone else? What are your impressions of those experiences?

_____

_____

_____

_____

_____

_____

_____

_____

Mentoring will address many areas of life. It will begin to break negative cycles, leading to a life of maturity, victory, and impact. I am convinced that this is God's plan for all Christians. Proverbs 27:17 (BSB) affirms, *"As iron sharpens iron, so one man sharpens another."* There is a human truth that people can accomplish more together than apart. Spiritually, you can achieve greater impact yoked beside somebody than as a single plow in the field.

Consider Jesus' ministry and how He prepared His apostles through regular instruction with a message that changed the world. It involved teaching, correcting, and encouraging with lots of patience over three full years. Jesus' mentoring was complete at that time, even while they themselves still had to mature. But He brought them to a place where they rightly understood who He was, His mission, their calling, and that they were equipped to fulfill it. Old patterns were broken in them; new wineskins were created. They accepted a new trajectory of life because of the investment of one Man. Such is the power of mentorship! **Mentoring is about keeping the cycle of success going.**

Paul described Timothy as his *"true son in the faith"* (1 Timothy 1:2, NIV). Paul had taken Timothy along on his third missionary journey, investing time, wisdom, instruction, and his own life into the young man. The mentee went on to become the pastor of the Ephesian church through the training he witnessed first-hand. Paul was a great example of forwarding to others what God poured into him. He was confident that he had received the Word, had matured in the ways of the Kingdom, and was walking in truth. So, he could rightly say, "Hey! Follow me as I follow Christ."

The apostle wrote in Philippians 4:9 (NLT): *"Keep putting into practice all you learned and received from me—everything you heard from me and saw me doing."* He further explains his method of mentorship by stating, *"We loved you so much that we shared with you not only God's Good News but our own lives too"* (1 Thessalonians 2:8, NLT). This type of teaching encapsulates what mentoring is all about—preparing others to love and obey the voice of God in every way possible in a world of compromise and sin.

Not only will mentoring break cycles of sin, but it will also produce eternal impact that the world so desperately needs!

Which person in your life currently is an example to you of how to remain near to Jesus? What does he or she do that strengthens your faith?

_____

_____

_____

_____

_____

_____

_____

_____

Mentorship involves opening our lives to others—discussing struggles, sharing experiences together, praying for one another, talking about family and work, loving each other through failures, and celebrating victories as a team. It is living life together to intentionally build God's Kingdom in others. Practically speaking, I believe there are 4 T's of mentoring.

The first T is **truth**—*the transference of truth*. When you mentor someone you take the wisdom and knowledge that was instilled in you, and you pass it on to other individuals. A second element is **trust**—*building a trusting relationship*. It is vital to create a non-judgmental, compassionate atmosphere for sharing that allows more intimate details to be discussed. A third T of mentoring is **transparency**—*inviting* *another to look at the typically hidden areas of your life.* These relationships permit others access to see and to hear the real you without hiding things. Lastly, mentoring involves **time**—*investing time for trust to build and change to occur.*

Mentoring with the same person doesn't last forever as seasons of life change, growth is achieved, and new friendships develop. It says that, for an amount of time, I commit to pouring into your life. But as God brings to light a person for you to live your life in front of and invest in, make the most of your time, however long it lasts. He wants to use you! On the other hand, Jesus makes a striking comparison for those who lead others astray with their influence.

Read Matthew 18:6. What does Jesus say about misusing our influence?

_____

_____

_____

_____

_____

_____

_____

When God brings people into our lives for us to influence, take it seriously. There is no room for taking advantage of them or pointing them away from full allegiance to Jesus. Mentoring is a privilege. An untold amount of Kingdom-sized good will flow from strong and patient mentoring.

GOING DEEPER

1. Who has the Lord brought into your circle of influence who you could invite to walk closer to you as you follow Jesus?

_____

_____

_____

_____

_____

_____

_____

2. How did Paul mentor others?

_____

_____

_____

_____

_____

_____

_____

CHAPTER 4

MENTORING: KEEPING IT GOING

"Once again Jesus went out beside the sea. All the people came to Him, and He taught them there. As He was walking along, He saw Levi son of Alphaeus sitting at the tax booth. 'Follow Me,' He told him, and Levi got up and followed Him."
—*Mark 2:13–14 (BSB)*

Mentoring is God's idea. Jesus did it. Paul did it. And countless other Christian leaders through the centuries have made spiritual mentorship a priority in their ministries that left profound generational impact across nations. This practice involves sharing one's life with another person, allowing him or her to have a clearer understanding of who you truly are, how you deal with stress, how you pray, when you spend time with the Lord in quiet time, and how you do it, how you lead others, how you trust the Lord with finances, and much more. Mentoring is keeping the cycle of success going. As leaders, you and I are called to this. It is the method God gave us to forward the change that He began.

What qualities would you like to see in someone that you mentor? Why?

_____

_____

_____

_____

_____

_____

_____

_____

Let's dig a little deeper into how to select someone to mentor. Consider the *character element*. You understand already that we can preach, teach, and warn a whole room of people, but we can't mentor everybody. You can only mentor a few individuals with your limited time, so refine your search parameters to narrow the options. When it comes to mentoring, we should look for a person who demonstrates hunger for change, to become more than what he or she already is, who wants to be used by God. A short-sighted person will not reach for more. Look for a person's drive to serve, encourage, love others, soak in, and pour out.

As a sidenote, I want to reiterate something: before you mentor someone, you must be a person of character yourself, a person of conviction, someone who can be an example to others. Does that mean you must be perfect with no flaws or hang-ups? No, it doesn't. But you are aware of them, confess them, and are actively growing in your personal holiness so that those shortcomings become less frequent and less powerful in you. Thank God that He uses broken vessels to still carry water! You've got to seek to be a person of godly character yourself. I like what Paul said: *"You have heard me teach things that have been confirmed by many reliable witnesses . . ."* (2 Timothy 2:2, NLT). Paul didn't have to hide or explain away what he had previously said or done. He was confident that it was truthful and had integrity—all of it.

What other qualities should we seek in someone to potentially mentor? One additional characteristic is a person's willingness to learn and grow. Some may be willing to receive information but do nothing with it. You want to identify people not only willing to learn, but willing to live it out. They ought to be willing to put in intentional effort to become a person of Christlike character, a person of righteousness and holiness.

As you invest in people, the goal is not just to instill more knowledge but to help develop in them the character of Christ.

How would you define a successful mentorship? What would be "achieved" or developed for you to consider it a "win"?

_____

_____

_____

_____

_____

_____

_____

Focus on the mind *and* the heart. Did Jesus love? Absolutely! Like no one ever has or ever will. In fact, this quality defines His disciples. Read John 13:35. Sharing unconditional love with others reveals His true character in a person. It surpasses mere tolerance; it extends its hand to demonstrate compassion and care for the souls of others without expecting anything in return. Leadership will flow naturally out of genuine love for people. This quality—loving like Jesus loved—is one that you want to help mature in a mentee.

Continuing with how to select someone to mentor, I believe it is the work of the Holy Spirit to bring people together. Have you ever been around certain individuals and suddenly it just *clicked?* God uses divine encounters to bring people together for purposes higher than we perceive. That person may not be who you would have chosen to mentor (or to mentor you) but you can't get around that special spiritual bond. Don't judge the book by its cover. He or she may be older chronologically, or younger chronologically, dress differently, or live on the other side of town, but don't rule them out. *"Man sees the outward appearance, but the Lord sees the heart"* (1 Samuel 16:7, BSB). We ought to ask the Lord to send people into our lives so we can pass on truth and godly wisdom. I'll tell you this—it will not be who you expect! But be available and ready when the Lord brings that person to you.

If you have mentored another before now, how did you feel about it at the beginning of that relationship and how did that feeling change over time?

_____

_____

_____

_____

_____

_____

_____

_____

_____

Let's add another layer to this mentorship topic—the **content element**. Don't just choose the right person; pass on the right Person. In mentoring, you're not reproducing yourself, developing someone who talks and acts just like you. Think long-term. It is not about you or me; it is about becoming more like Jesus. What your home, your church, and your community need is more of Christ in you. The true content, or what it is we're passing on, consists not of what I feel or think, what I ate for breakfast, or my experiences. It consists of communicating the truth about Jesus Christ, the eternal Savior revealed in the Bible.

Our content is Him and His Word. Choose readings that bring that person into God's Word, and then talk about it.

What book(s) of the Bible would you want to read first with a mentee?

_____

_____

_____

_____

_____

If we demonstrate and duplicate falling in love with Jesus and aligning our lives under His Lordship, then we have succeeded at mentorship! There is a lifetime of learning how to walk obediently and intimately with Him, and a mentor should walk with others along that path. We are messengers who pass on these truths to others, ultimately helping to develop a heart of obedient love for the Savior.

A third component of mentorship is what I call the *chance element.* This speaks of the transparency needed to lead others, as well as the uncertainty involved. How many times have we tried to muscle through life in our own human power and gifts, according to our own wisdom and clever rationale? **None of us can lead others spiritually without God's empowerment and direction that are found as we humble ourselves in His presence.** We recognize that, without His grace, we are inadequate to lead others well. Such a spirit enables us to confidently live a life of transparency. Paul told Timothy, *"My dear son, be strong through the grace that God gives you in Christ Jesus"* (2 Timothy

2:1, NLT). We can only do it if we are living in the grace and strength that comes from Jesus Christ. Otherwise, it is like trying to pour water from a dry cup.

"Lord, keep me humble, seeing my need for You, Your grace, and Your wisdom. Strengthen me to live a transparent life before You so that I can lead a transparent life before others."

As you can imagine, this is also the reality of ministry that every leader faces. In 2 Timothy 1:15 (NLT), Paul writes, *"As you know, everyone from the province of Asia has deserted me, even Phygelus and Hermogenes."* As you read Paul's encounters in subsequent chapters, a man named Demas deserted him because he loved the things of life more than the Savior, and Alexander the coppersmith did him much harm.

You can help people, reach out to them, be nice and kind, and still get hurt by them. Nevertheless, God commands us to take that chance and keep on pouring into their lives to expand God's Kingdom. The truth is that you can choose certain people, pour your life into them, and they still may end up rejecting your hand of investment.

When it comes to mentoring it's about choosing to make time for it. It is putting in the time for the things that matter most—investments in eternity, helping to develop minds and souls. **Many of us are living lives that we never thought we would live. We are doing things we never thought we would do. Now God is saying it's your time for that next step of mentoring.** It's your time to invest in somebody else. It's your time to help bring up somebody else. It's your time to train up the next generation.

Open up your eyes and look for some potential in others. Look for that boy or that girl. Let them know, "I've been there and done that.

I can show you a better way and His name is Jesus and His instructions are for your good." Then *open up your heart* in order to love them. Be willing to share your life and be vulnerable. "I'm going to open my heart and let you into my life. I'm going to let you ask me questions and I commit to help you on your journey. Then *open up your mouth* to speak truth. When you're mentoring someone, you must be willing to tell him or her the truth. Then *open up your life* so they can see the truth lived out in you.

Break the cycle and create new cycles of discipline, self-control, Bible reading, service, compassion, rejoicing, fellowship, and faithfulness . . . not just in you, but in the one in your life who also needs it!

When Jesus comes back, hear him say, "Servant, well done! You made disciples. You warned others. You invested time. You poured your life into others. You helped train up somebody else." Sitting quietly in your seat is no longer an option. Forwarding the change is the responsibility of us all!

GOING DEEPER

1. If you could pass on anything to someone you mentor, what qualities or truths would be most important?

_____

_____

_____

_____

_____

_____

2. What is the most intimidating part of spiritual mentoring to you?

_____

_____

_____

_____

_____

_____

3. Who could you look to as an example of godly mentorship to you?

_____

_____

_____

_____

_____

4. What changes in your life would have to be made to make room for mentoring?

_____

_____

_____

_____

_____

_____

_____

_____

FEARLESS CHANGE

CHAPTER 5

MISSIONS: MAKING IT FULFILLING

"Among the prophets and teachers of the church at Antioch of Syria were Barnabas, Simeon (called "the black man"), Lucius (from Cyrene), Manaen (the childhood companion of King Herod Antipas), and Saul. One day as these men were worshiping the Lord and fasting, the Holy Spirit said, 'Appoint Barnabas and Saul for the special work to which I have called them.' So after more fasting and prayer, the men laid their hands on them and sent them on their way."
—Acts 13:1-3 (NLT)

What a church the Antioch of Syria church was! This group of Christ-followers was a mission-minded, Spirit-filled church, birthed amidst persecution and suffering. After the martyrdom of Stephen in Jerusalem, we read that nearly all Christians were severely persecuted and scattered abroad, talking about Jesus wherever they went (Acts 8). Through these uprooted men, women, and children, the message about Jesus soon arrived in Antioch of Syria, just north of Israel. The church there was birthed during a time of struggle among an ungodly population. Antioch was a corrupt, pagan city. Yet the Christian congregation was able to become firmly established and thrive, rising above prejudice, pettiness, hatred, and hostility. Antioch would soon become a church that would literally impact the world with the gospel of Jesus Christ.

What role should a local church have in supporting missions?

_____

_____

_____

_____

_____

_____

With my own congregation, I often refer to the 6 G's that should define every church, the responsibilities of every local fellowship. We see these qualities demonstrated in the life of the Antioch church, and I believe they serve as guideposts to extending that which God entrusted to His people. Christ longs for His church to become healthy and stay vitalized, enabling her to be in a continual state of readiness to go on mission.

First, Antioch proved itself to be a *genuine* church. Look how the Bible describes it in Acts 11:21 (NLT): *"The power of the Lord was with them, and a large number of these Gentiles believed and turned to the Lord."* When those traveling with the Gospel arrived and proclaimed the truth in Antioch, genuine conversions took place. People were sure about their salvation! News of such rapid growth in the church traveled to Jerusalem, moving leaders to send Barnabas to investigate (v.22). You can imagine that the people of Antioch were listening to the words of these visiting Christians, recognizing their lifestyles, their conviction, their integrity, which gave credence to their message. The new believers started living out the truths of what they heard, learning to live as holy children of God. God's favor was upon them. **Genuine salvation produce fruit that is evident for others to see.**

When you consider what a genuine church looks like, what qualities come to mind?

_____

_____

_____

_____

_____

_____

Not only genuine, but Antioch was a *growing* church. Acts 11:26 tells that for a whole year, Barnabas and Saul (also known as Paul) stayed with the church, teaching large crowds of people. In this city, it began with a large number of salvations and continued to grow in number over many months. While it is not said in this passage, it is possible that these Christians met very often together. The first-century church was described as meeting together daily to share meals, pray, learn the apostles' teaching, and to fellowship (Acts 2:42). Not a bad recipe for growth! Multiplication is inevitable when Christians genuinely love each other, walk in unity, learn God's Word, seek Him in prayer, and whose lives match the faith they profess. I wonder how our churches would expand wider and deeper if this became a more regular practice among us.

Thirdly, Antioch was a *giving* church. Together, they prepared and sent gifts to brothers and sisters in Judea whom they had never met, inviting Paul and Barnabas to deliver them. Money is just one aspect of giving. People need food. People need services done at their homes, like repairs, grass to be mowed, and floors to be vacuumed. God's people need to be generous givers in whatever capacities they are capable. *"Therefore, whenever we have the opportunity, we should do good to everyone—especially to those in the family of faith"* (Galatians 6:10, NLT).

What are some examples of *giving* that Christians could do in neighborhoods and communities to bring Christ to the people in practical ways?

_____

_____

_____

_____

_____

_____

_____

_____

_____

Next, it was a *gifted* church. Antioch was filled with men and women who lived in the power of the Holy Spirit, sensitive to His leadings. We see in Acts 13:1-3 that prophets and teachers were present among the large group of believers, and that there was fasting and praying. The Spirit does not force Himself on anyone; it is our choice to yield to Him. *"Since we are living by the Spirit, let us follow the Spirit's leading in every part of our lives"* (Galatians 5:25, NLT). Each of us must choose at the beginning of the day, and throughout the day, to follow His leading. **Mission-mindedness is responding to the instructions of God's Word and promptings of the Holy Spirit.**

Every time we use these gifts, it better equips and encourages God's people. When one person decides not to share that gift, the whole body suffers. Paul elaborates on this truth in 1 Corinthians 12 when comparing the church and the gifts to a human body. Every part is essential to the full functioning of the body. Like Antioch, we are part of gifted churches. **As leaders, we must continue to call people up to a higher vision that their unique gifts do matter, that they play an important role in the health of the whole body.** Read Romans 12:3-8.

What are some gifts that the Holy Spirit gives to Christians as means of strengthening others?

_____

_____

_____

_____

_____

_____

_____

_____

_____

_____

Furthermore, Antioch was a *graceful* church. Showing others grace involves much more than simply being nice. Being a gracious person begins deep within the heart where sincere love for others is the extensive root system. From those roots of love blossom words, attitudes, and actions of grace. This begins with Christ in us, who is the Hope of Glory. *"We love because He first loved us"* (1 John 4:19, BSB).

A final distinguishing quality was that they were a *going* church. Acts 13:2-3 explains that they were worshipping and fasting, and the Holy Spirit revealed that Barnabas and Paul were to leave their church for "a special work" to which He called them. The church's response? To support the Spirit's leading. A going church recognizes God's calling to "Go"—away from what is known and comfortable—and supports that calling with prayer and resources. The challenge falls in not attempting to "intervene" with human reason, which has deflated many Christians with visions of spreading the Gospel. Antioch sensitively and fearlessly responded to God's leading, supporting, and resourcing Barnabas and Paul to fulfill that calling. Little did any of them know the surpassing impact that this support would have on the known world!

Paul returned to report to his home church what God had done, then they supported him on his second and third missionary journeys. Antioch literally became the sending church that had the most far-reaching impact for the name of Jesus. This was a church that was so fired up about missions that they did not mind sacrificing one of their leading teaching pastors for the sake of the Gospel.

The Lord has called us to go into all the world to preach and teach new believers the commands He gave, while giving us confidence with the knowledge that He is always with us, even unto the end of the world (Matthew 28:20). A mission-minded church is genuine, growing, giving, gifted, graceful, and going.

GOING DEEPER

1. Which qualities of the church at Antioch are most inspiring to you?

_____

_____

_____

_____

_____

_____

2. How would you respond if the Lord clearly revealed to you to go on mission locally, regionally, or internationally?

_____

_____

_____

_____

_____

_____

_____

_____

3. What gifts do you believe the Spirit has given you and how are you using your gifts to strengthen your local church?

_____

_____

_____

_____

_____

_____

_____

_____

CHAPTER 6

MISSIONS: MAKING IT FAR-REACHING

"The Lord is not slow in keeping His promise
as some understand slowness, but is patient
with you, not wanting anyone to perish
but everyone to come to repentance."
—2 Peter 3:9 (BSB)

There are some things that we ought to do *inside* the church to prepare us for what God has called us to do *outside* the church. We must equip the church body inside the walls so that we can do the work of the church outside the walls. We will keep worshiping here so that we can be witnessing out there. We've got to stay fired up in the church so we can burn for Jesus in the streets. It is small-minded to believe that God's work is only for a select group who meet inside the church walls. Yes, when we gather, it is the time and place to stoke the fire and become equipped. We come to be revived and prepared inside so we can be passionate out there. Sunday mornings and other mid-week gatherings are the moments to be trained, schooled, and encouraged by other saints. **But these "inside" experiences are not the end goal. They prepare us to live out God's mission to our world and make an "outside impact."**

Think of a time at church where you sensed God's presence. How did that experience affect your willingness to obey Him?

_____

_____

_____

_____

_____

_____

_____

What He pours in, we must pour out. The work God does within us is meant to be far-reaching in its scope. Every church must follow the principle in 2 Corinthians 1:4 (NLT). Paul writes, *"He comforts us in all our troubles so that we can comfort others."* What principle is he sharing with his readers? Simply, the blessings, wisdom, and comfort that He has entrusted to us through difficult circumstances do not belong just to us; they are intended to be a blessing to others. In short, we are blessed to be a blessing! Read Genesis 12:1-3.

What principle did God convey to Abram?

_____

_____

_____

_____

_____

_____

_____

It is simple: we are blessed to be a blessing. For the Lord's Kingdom to expand beyond our Christian circles, we must go and we must give! Father God wishes *"none to perish but everyone to come to repentance"* (2 Peter 3:9). Churches and individuals must not ignore these clear instructions to move out of a comfortable routine and remember that souls are lost and people need Jesus all around us. For God's mission to the world to continue expanding, we each can take three actions.

First, we keep ***praying for focus.*** I call this the need for *the right destination.* Often, we have agendas, but they are not the Lord's agenda, or our ideas of progress but not His ideas. We need to pray for clearer focus, beginning with, "Lord, not my will but Yours be done." One of the things I like about the church at Antioch is that they sought God for His will to be clarified and confirmed. **They put their "Yes" on the table and truly yielded their next step to their Commander-in-Chief.** And with that next step, they stepped out in faith.

Let us pray that God will give us focus for what he has called us to do in our communities and world. There is no shortage of opportunity, so we need the Lord to lead. God calls us to simply follow the directions and trust His plan. God sent Paul and Barnabas on this first journey, then Paul and Silas on the second and third trips. Where is God leading you? Your church? To whom is God sending you? What work has He been leading you to do? Pray for focus then follow the directions.

As you pray for focus, keep *paying for funds*. How in the world is this church going to be able to keep sending Paul out on missionary journeys? I believe it is, in part, because some Christians in Antioch supported him financially for the cause of Christ. As those individuals were not called by the Spirit to go, they participated in missions by funding those who were impressed to go. If God has blessed us, He has blessed us to be a blessing to others. In the Antioch church, everybody gave as much as they were able, whether little or much, because they recognized it all came from God. And if it all came from God, it all belongs to Him to move around as He sees the need. Therefore, we give cheerfully to the Lord's work knowing that we all have a part to play to "go and tell."

God has sufficient resources and fully knows the needs that His people have. Consider 2 Corinthians 9:6-7 (NLT): *"A farmer who plants only a few seeds will get a small crop. But the one who plants generously will get a generous crop. You must each decide in your heart how much to give. And don't give reluctantly or in response to pressure."* Paul follows that illustration with an assurance.

Read v. 8 and write what it states in your own words.

_____

_____

_____

_____

_____

_____

_____

Third, we keep ***praising for favor***. As the Antioch leaders worshipped the Lord and fasted, the Holy Spirit appointed Barnabas and Silas for the work to which He called them. It happened during their worship, their church service. When we have decisions to make or questions that need answers, this is the time to worship, not worry. In joining the Body of Christ as a unified group of worshippers, we experience the fullness of the Holy Spirit, teaching from the Word, and godly community. These help to realign us with His will and refuel us to return to our individual local mission fields.

Praising at church is like burning coals that give strength and heat to one another, as we come to get fired up and to get our marching orders. When we praise God in spirit and in truth no matter the circumstances, I believe the favor of God will show up. May our churches live in this same spirit and expectation of hearing from Him as we worship.

God is calling us to come inside, to get some healing, to receive some instruction and correction, to be refreshed and refilled by the Spirit. Keep your fire burning on the inside. Be consistent to worship and fast from certain things in this world to be the sharpest sword that God can use at any moment. To become and stay on mission to build Christ's Kingdom, we must nourish our own souls in His presence, with His people, and in His Word.

GOING DEEPER

1. What routines and habits do you have to refuel your spiritual life?

_____

_____

_____

_____

_____

_____

_____

2. How have you implemented the principle of "You are blessed to be a blessing"? What are other ways to be a blessing to build Christ's Kingdom?

_____

_____

_____

_____

_____

_____

_____

3. How has the Lord stretched you to trust Him in your giving to the church and to missions?

_____

_____

_____

_____

_____

_____

_____

CHAPTER 7

MINISTRY: MAKING IT KNOWN

"Jesus traveled throughout the region of Galilee, teaching in the synagogues and announcing the Good News about the Kingdom. And He healed every kind of disease and illness. News about Him spread as far as Syria, and people soon began bringing to Him all who were sick. And whatever their sickness or disease, or if they were demon possessed or epileptic or paralyzed—He healed them all. Large crowds followed Him wherever He went—people from Galilee, the Ten Towns, Jerusalem, from all over Judea, and from east of the Jordan River ...

When He saw the crowds, He had compassion on them because they were confused and helpless, like sheep without a shepherd. He said to his disciples, "The harvest is great, but the workers are few. So pray to the Lord who is in charge of the harvest, ask Him to send more workers into His fields."
—Matthew 4:23–25; 9:36–38 (NLT)

Perhaps you have watched individuals, churches, and Christian organizations serve and gradually developed your own ideas of what would be most effective for your own ministry. And it works. It's good. Nothing stellar but it works. I wonder, though, if the Lord wants to reveal more than what's always been done, more than what is realistic from our perspective. Something richer, deeper, and impactful. Let's consider how Jesus did ministry. Before that, though, consider what not to do.

In Isaiah 58:3-10, the Lord explained to the Jewish people through the prophet that they did worshipful deeds, but it was flawed. Read this passage and describe what God wanted from His people.

_____

_____

_____

_____

_____

_____

Churches need to be aware of making certain things the main thing that shouldn't be the main thing, and forgetting other things that should be the main thing. The problem is when we sing, pray, and dance while the poor, widows, and orphans long for some compassion and assistance. Hungry people still need groceries. Is the church pursuing justice for the oppressed, speaking for hurting communities? In our freedom of worship, are we forgetting or ignoring the plight of those in need outside our church doors?

The Lord challenges us to take up the Word and a shovel, and do the work of ministry outside of the church walls. That leads us to Jesus' words and actions in Matthew 4. I see several practical insights here to move us beyond what we view as acceptable ministry to "Outside the Box" ministry.

First, we see Jesus' *motivation*. What moved Jesus? I believe it was His desire to bring wholeness and significance to each person. This speaks of his rich compassion for their eternal souls, weighted minds, and broken bodies. *"When He saw the crowds, He had compassion on them because they were confused and helpless"* (Matthew 9:36, NLT). He looked around and saw, not a crowd, but individuals with names who had deep spiritual and physical needs. Likewise, the people around us are emotionally exhausted, even within a life of comfort they made for themselves. They are spiritually separated from God. Individuals back then and today are lost sheep in need of a shepherd to meet those God-shaped holes.

The sad thing about us today is that some of us have lost our compassion and heart for the downtrodden. All ministry is birthed out of genuine compassion for others in need. Too often we are moved by songs than we are by lost souls, or moved by the band, but not by the brokenness around us. Why doesn't the church serve more in our schools, community centers, shelters, or local ministries? Could it be due to a lack of compassion? People say that they make time for what is most important to them. Is showing practical compassion not a priority any longer?

What are some reasons that Christians do not regularly minister to others outside the church?

_____

_____

_____

_____

_____

_____

_____

_____

Second, I see the ***mobilization*** of Jesus. I call this His concentration because of where Jesus chose to work. Often when churches begin thinking about ministry, we try to limit it to certain places or people. I don't see that in Jesus's life. The Bible said that He and His disciples traveled throughout the region of Galilee, Judean, and even Samaria. He didn't just stay in His comfortable office chair but made it a priority to go where people needed His touch. His mobilization was everywhere. God wants to expand the way we think about ministry—we can't limit it to certain places.

What has been God's mission for His church since its inception? Go everywhere! Jesus is recorded in Acts 1:8 (BSB) saying, *"You will be My witnesses in Jerusalem, and in all Judea and Samaria, and to the ends of the earth."* That's exactly what His disciples did. They spread across what we know as northern Africa, to Spain and parts of Europe, all the way east to India. They clearly got His mission and acted on it.

There will always be differences in where we minister. Let's not judge where the Lord has led individuals and churches to minister but rather celebrate their specific focus, while we focus on where God leads *us*. It may center on one or two areas, or in a multitude of areas. But let there not be a restriction on where we are willing to go for Him. **God wants us to go across the street and across the water. He wants us to go around the corner and up and down the highway. He wants us to go everywhere. Don't limit it according to the place or preconceived notions.**

Oh, I'm glad that Jesus didn't set parameters on who He served! When it came to ministry, He served everybody. Even when a Syrophoenician woman, a Gentile, came to Him to explain her daughter was vexed with a demon, Jesus graciously chose to deliver the young girl (Mark 7:24-30). Why? His motivation was to show compassion, and His mobilization was everywhere and everybody! It could be you, or your church, who the Savior uses to reach a person, community, school, fire department, or entire region that no one has adequately served.

What is one area that you recognize needs the influence and ministry of Christians?

_____

_____

_____

_____

_____

_____

Third, we look at His **methods**. Throughout the Gospels, we read over and over that Jesus came to preach, teach, and heal. I call this the complete cure—service in not just one area, but all three. Paul describes this concept of wholistic ministry in 1 Thessalonians 5:23 (NIV): *"May God himself, the God of peace, sanctify you through and through."* I believe that preaching, teaching, and healing will serve each one of those—body, soul, and spirit. Recall that Jesus healed sick and broken bodies. He also was about feeding the hungry. It is hard to convince crowds of the provision of the Bread of Life when their stomachs are hungry. Ministry must not ignore this area while it also cares for spiritual health. God compassionately restored many bodies, and still does today within His divine plan.

Paul also mentioned the health of the human soul. The Lord desires people to experience mental and emotional well-being. If you want peace of mind, stability in your emotions, or to change your perspective, God's truths are available in scripture to act as salve, medicine, and therapy. The truths of God in the Bible—instructions, promises, warnings, encouragement, wisdom, and assurances—are His methods to restore what has been beaten, bent, and broken over the years. Teaching these truths administers healing to our emotional and mental wounds. As you and I let people know what He has said, we will witness more people set free! And those who are free can, in turn, set others free.

Not only healing for the body and teaching for our mind, but God also gave us preaching for the spirit. While some may view the difference between teaching and preaching as just semantics, I refer to the spirit as that part of us that responds to God Almighty in relationship, with preaching as the means of touching the spirit. This component of one's being is what distinguishes humans from other parts of creation. Preaching helps connect us with God. Let's make sure we preach the full Gospel and get people saved. Each person longs to be in intimate relationship with their Creator but many are not yet aware of it, and God has called us to make them aware. Preaching the Gospel clearly and often is a core element of ministry and must never be pushed aside. A well-fed belly can still end up in hell. Let's preach the Good News of Jesus in season and out of season.

The last observation from this passage involves what I call the *multitudes*. Matthew 4:25 says large crowds followed him wherever he went—people from Galilee, from the Ten Towns, from Jerusalem, all over Judea, and from the east of the Jordan River. They were coming from everywhere like sheep—broken, lost, and confused—searching for a shepherd, and a good one. The crowds found Him. Would they find us just as ready to receive them, broken and dusty, looking for acknowledgment of their worth and healing for their whole beings? **Often, we show up for ministry because we like being able to control the extent of it, but sometimes ministry shows up at our door without notice. Is our response like that of our Savior?**

Who do you know who accepts interruptions graciously as opportunities to minister to others? How can you better imitate this quality?

_____

_____

_____

_____

Citywide, statewide, and worldwide ministry is too much for any one person or church to handle. Each of us does a little . . . and much gets done. Thank God for the crowds. They reveal that our hands, words, hearts, time, resources, and efforts are still desperately needed. Crowds remind us that the world is still broken and in need of holistic healing in the name of Jesus. Crowds remind us that there is more to do. "Lord, what can I do to heal broken bodies, souls, and spirits in Your name?"

God wants a crowd. Consider the parable Jesus told of the man who threw a wedding feast, who told his servants to go inform all those previously invited that the preparations were ready at last. After guests declined, more were invited. Yet there was still more room in the house. *"Go out to the highways and hedges and compel them to come in, so that my house will be full,"* was the instruction (Luke 14:15-23, BSB). Do you see the heart of God? He wants a crowd. He wants a crowd because He is not willing that any should perish but that all should come to repentance. **If we do what God has called us to do, I believe not only will we go *to the crowd*, but the crowd will want to *come to us*.**

And when the crowd comes to you, let's not label the new people who are checking out what we have going on. We mustn't shun the lost just because they don't have it all together. Then again, do we? We can't say, "They're newcomers and I don't like newcomers, or the way they dress, or how they talk! . . ." Embrace the crowd because the Lord wants everybody to meet Him. Our selfishness and judgment keep us in the box while God is outside our religious box wanting us to introduce them to Him. Until they meet Him, they are looking at you and your church family. We've got to get this right or they won't be returning next week . . . or maybe ever.

A living example of this principle was depicted in the movie "Jesus Revolution," with Pastor Chuck Smith learning to embrace an eccentric, earthly group of young people in society called "hippies." This group longed for meaning in life and to connect with God, albeit through sex, drugs, and rock-and-roll. Pastor Chuck realized that the traditional ranks of the church rejected hippies, and he was one of them for a season. But God helped him to cross the bridge to meet these hippies, listen to them, invite them, involve them, love them, and preach to them. His church began with 25 members in Costa Mesa, California in 1965 and grew into a network of over 1,000 Calvary Chapel churches across the world. Pastor Chuck's ministry expanded outside the box, leading to a wave of nationwide spiritual awakening unrivaled since then . . . all because one man chose to do ministry like Jesus did it.

When it comes to ministry, the church can't stay inside the four walls of the church. **God is patiently, yet firmly telling us to get outside the box, to reimagine what we view as realistic.** While maturity within the church body and serving our own people are essential, some are only trying to help that group. Think beyond the walls. What can you offer Him to use? Following Jesus requires getting outside the box. I pray that we will forever be a church that thinks beyond ourselves.

GOING DEEPER

1. What are some "main things" that individuals and churches should focus on in ministry? What are some lesser important preferences that shouldn't make that list?

_____

_____

_____

_____

_____

_____

2. What kinds of healing does God want to give to people?

_____

_____

_____

_____

_____

3. What groups of people are being overlooked for ministry in your area? How can you intervene, even in a small way?

_____

_____

_____

_____

_____

_____

FRUITFUL CHANGE

CHAPTER 8

MULTIPLY: MAXIMIZING THE MISSION

"And no one puts new wine into old wineskins.
For the wine would burst the wineskins, and
the wine and the skins would both be lost.
New wine calls for new wineskins."
—*Mark 2:22 (NLT)*

The mission of the church never changes, but methods do.

Pastors and leaders must face a reality—the world has changed, and with it the people. There are mental and emotional filters in our communities that spiritual leaders today must recognize and confront. Pastors must consider the cultural mentality of twenty-first century Americans as they are preparing strategic communications for their ministries. But the foundational mission remains the same: share the Gospel of Jesus, disciple God's people, care for the church, and serve the community. The methods we use, however, must change for the church to continue being relevant and effective.

What are some changes that you have observed in churches over the years?

_____

_____

_____

_____

_____

_____

_____

_____

The people sitting before us each week are not the same as a few decades ago. They have become increasingly accustomed to short soundbites of information, the use of personal stories to validate a topic, the comfort and efficiency of smartphones, digital communication, a slice of entertainment from presenters, a customer mentality, opportunities to use or add to their social media feeds, and more. Leaders must ponder each of these experiences as we think forward to not just this year, but to one, five, and ten years from now. As you have insights and ideas for potential changes, remember that changes are most successful when made gradually and with a coalition of leaders.

For now, let's look at various areas of ministry and how some churches have carefully thought through these considerations.

DIGITAL MARKETING

People are used to learning about virtually anything through searching the Internet, which includes the church they will visit. When looking at your church website, seekers (both Christians and non-Christians) will make a judgment about your church based on what they see and hear. Because people want to get a quick snapshot of a church, they may decide to continue investigating your church from a quick perusal of that front webpage. Make that page count!

Integrating social media is huge and is already embraced by many in your church population. Use this tool strategically! Post recent pictures on the church's social media sites. Include short videos on Instagram and Facebook of the pastor introducing the church with a brief introduction and invitation. This is a perfect platform for posting important announcements, a new sermon series, or an invitation to a special event with the use of professional graphics.

Regular posts help keep church events in front of your members, allowing them to "like" it and share it with their spheres of influence. What a way for your church family to invite their friends next week!

Start small and do it well. Social media is powerful and is where many "share life" with others, and that life should involve your church. In addition, video is extremely effective to convey information. Think of fifteen-second or thirty-second commercials—essential advertising for companies. While churches are not for-profit organizations, they ought to integrate videos more regularly to explain what good things are happening. Remember that people should be told something a few times and in a few ways to help it stay in their memories. Let videos become one of those components of communication that builds excitement.

Imagine playing a short video montage with overlaid music before the service starts as a means of introducing the church to attendees and as a reminder that the service is about to start. Another church may use a picture montage of how the church has served others before extending the invitation to give. Make a lasting impression. Show them who you are!

How can you integrate videos into your service or improve your current video usage?

_____

_____

_____

_____

_____

_____

_____

_____

In addition, because our culture is often too impatient to read a whole article about a topic, they'll defer to something that is a bite-sized read. Enter tweeting. Members of churches will post a memorable quote to their friend network from the pastor's sermon as a snapshot of Sunday morning. As a result of that post, those readers whose interest is piqued can follow an embedded hyperlink to the recorded church service and/or website. Make it easier for your own people, and those looking in from the outside, to get to know you. When you plant seeds in a variety of locations and platforms, there is more likelihood of fruitfulness from those places. Digital marketing in today's culture cannot be overstated. It combines the call to "Go and tell" with "Come and see."

ADMINISTRATIVE COMMUNICATION

Always keeping in mind that people today prefer the ease of completing tasks from their smartphones, pastors and leaders can use this device for administrative purposes within the church experience. Studies have found that providing an option for individuals to tithe from their phones increases the number of contributions received. Why? For a large percentage of our population, it is more preferable to click a few buttons from their seats than to write a check or drop cash into a container.

We live in a convenience culture. But some congregations integrate all options—plate, phone, and giving kiosks—to appeal to varying audiences. We want to meet people where they are, while providing various methods to do so.

Do you use online giving methods at your church? Is it a tool that you would value exploring?

_____

_____

_____

_____

_____

_____

_____

_____

_____

Connection cards were created for congregants to communicate for various reasons on a physical card, which they would drop off in the giving area or at a welcome center. What if you provided a way for people to communicate with the church leadership in other ways—perhaps from the convenience of their phones? Some churches regularly display and refer to a specific phone number to text that pulls up information about the church, events, a link to tithe, a link to submit a prayer request or praise report, and to volunteer for an upcoming event. The possibilities are endless.

MINISTRY TOOLS

How can you serve your church after they leave the church parking lot? Consider the inputs that will strengthen their spiritual growth—God's Word, worship songs, prayer, fellowship. Could the use of technology assist in individuals' spiritual development? Remember that every week, thousands of churches stream their services that are viewed by individuals in 200 countries around the world. The Gospel is getting out quicker than ever before. Praise the Lord! Let your message be one of them through sharing the URL links for others to access and then share. I also love what some church leaders decided to do in creating worship set lists and distributing those links on social media platforms, YouTube, and music streaming apps, like Spotify, Apple Music, or YouTube Music. Now you can find podcasts, sermon audio, and your church's favorite songs individually or as a collection.

FELLOWSHIP AND FUN

Not all great ministry ideas involve digital technology! There is no replacement for in-person smiles, hugs, and fun. Let's make getting together more enjoyable with some memorable experiences. People love food. Why not have a coffee budget before or after service with snacks? Churches will sometimes announce that they've grilled hot dogs and hamburgers outside and invite everyone to stick around and hang out. Of course, music also helps create a fun atmosphere before and after the worship service. Consider setting up a photo booth with a nice backdrop and some props. Many people love to take "selfie" and "friendsie" photos to capture a memory. Give people reasons to hang out before and after the service to encourage deeper connections with others. Ask those who are gifted at talking with others to interact with individuals and introduce them to one another. Research has shown that guests make their decision to return within the first few minutes of driving onto the church property. Let's make it memorable!

What are some ideas that you think would create a more engaging environment and encourage people to hang out before or after a worship service?

_____

_____

_____

_____

_____

_____

_____

_____

_____

SERVICE/VOLUNTEERS

One area of leadership that I believe all churches could improve upon is in the arena of volunteer relationships. The oil of the church is its volunteers, and they truly give a lot to make the church run smoothly. We need them. Therefore, we need to make much of them, and do it often! Celebrate these people every week in some manner. Speak words of encouragement and life into them privately and publicly as you see them pouring out. The most simple and sincere, "Thank you... We couldn't do this without you!" goes a very long way to inspire and strengthen others.

One church I know calls its volunteers the Dream Team. The church provides breakfast for them before they serve and showers them with recognition on Sunday mornings and beyond. This type of honor inspires them to continue and motivates others to get involved who are merely taking up air every week with no involvement. Even more, invite one or two volunteers to share what serving has meant to them in front of the congregation, or by video for the shy ones. New volunteers breathe fresh life into a group. Help make that happen through your intentional appreciation.

NEXT STEPS

Let's finish off with how to transition people into the next stage of involvement. There should be a regular invitation from the leadership for those who are new and those on the sidelines, so to speak, to take the next step of faith within the church with a clear roadmap of how to do it. Because this step is often scary for many people, it should not be difficult. Have a clearly defined space for someone to meet a hospitable leader who is friendly and knowledgeable of upcoming opportunities. Talk it up! The occasional testimony of a member who already went through the "Next Steps" event strengthens the resolve of those who are putting off the decision.

Signing up should be quick and easy at a table, kiosk, or by texting the church's designated number. Keep in mind that people make judgments of events based on the person they interact with, for good or for bad. Choose that person carefully. Of course, be the one who exemplifies excitement about how God is moving in your church and why you think that the others should get involved to experience more. Your enthusiasm is contagious!

I want to challenge you to evaluate your communication, marketing, and ministries. Could these become more accessible for your church members? Are there methods you can adjust to meet people where they are at? Don't get me wrong—our goal is never to water down God's truth. We are simply trying to create additional bridges for our community to walk over, other lines of communication, and means of connecting with us. These are some of the twenty-first century's new wineskins that we either use as tools, or potentially lose relevance with a large portion of our population. Change is healthy!

GOING DEEPER

1. How would you rate your church's use of social media and of texting? Is it worth investing in ways to enhance this in your church?

_____

_____

_____

_____

_____

_____

_____

_____

2. Challenge your team (and yourself) to investigate other churches' websites and social media presence to gain ideas of how to implement certain ideas into your toolbelt.

_____

_____

_____

_____

_____

_____

_____

_____

3. Who are the "creatives" in your church family who could help brainstorm how to reach and connect others in your community to your church fellowship through memorable activities and productions?

_____

_____

_____

_____

_____

_____

_____

_____

CHAPTER 9

MARVEL TOGETHER: POWERFUL CELEBRATION

*"I will sing to the LORD, for He is highly exalted.
The horse and rider He has thrown into the sea. The
LORD is my strength and my song, and He has
become my salvation. He is my God, and I will praise
Him, my father's God, and I will exalt Him . . ."*
—Exodus 15:1-2 (BSB)

Throughout the Old Testament and New Testament, we read of victories won by the Hebrew nation or by the newly birthed Christian community. Some victories came in battle; some were from the hundreds and thousands that came to faith in Christ through the Gospel; some involved signs and wonders done in the name of Jesus. There is something powerful when a group sets its focus to achieve a common goal. If you've ever participated in a team sport, you understand! We strategize as a group, pay close attention to the game, yell encouragement at teammates to prod them to give their all, clap at the success of someone's great performance, and finally celebrate together with hollers and shouts at a win.

Can't the same enthusiasm swell up in churches? I believe the impetus of celebration among Christians is gratitude to God and delighting in Him often. In case you, or your church family, need a few reasons to rejoice, allow me to list a few for you. Most importantly, God has forgiven every wicked sin of His followers, declared them innocent, holy, and adopted into His family forever. Celebrate! The King has assured glorious citizenship in His heaven that is beyond beauty and comprehension. Celebrate! In our hardest moments of life, His presence is our rest, deliverance, and hope because He is working all things for His good on our behalf. Celebrate! The Good Father has assembled a body of believers called the Church to be His physical representation on this planet to support and strengthen one another—a growing new family! Celebrate! And He has instilled in His people the Holy Spirit to lead, teach, empower, and encourage us in all seasons. Oh, celebrate with me, someone!

What makes you celebrate in your Christian faith?

_____

_____

_____

_____

_____

_____

_____

_____

We each have countless more reasons to praise Him independently and collectively. So why don't we do it more? Think about it for a second. . . . Why don't you celebrate His victories in your life more often and with more joy? It is not because there aren't reasons to celebrate. It is not wrong to get excited in church. Perhaps, as Jesus explained in the Parable of the Sower, our life is being choked by life's worries, seeking wealth, and pursuing pleasures (Matthew 13:22). Maybe we've lost our focus on His work and victories. **I believe that God's people are called to marvel together at what our King has done, is doing, and will do.**

The writer tells in Exodus 14:31-15:1-2 (BSB), *"When Israel saw the great power that the LORD had exercised over the Egyptians, the people feared the LORD and believed in Him and in His servant Moses. Then Moses and the Israelites sang this song to the LORD:*

"I will sing to the LORD,
　　for He is highly exalted.
The horse and rider

He has thrown into the sea.

The LORD is my strength and my song,

and He has become my salvation.

He is my God, and I will praise Him,

my father's God, and I will exalt Him ..."

All the people sang together. Then Miriam kept the celebration going, grabbed a timbrel, led the other women, and sang aloud for all to hear (Exodus 15:20-21).

Upon rebuilding the wall around Jerusalem in the face of opposition, the Jewish exiles finished and began their celebration together. Read Nehemiah 12:43. That's my kind of people! Can you sense their awe of God and His work, as well as their elation at this group victory? God enabled a new season to begin in the life of the Jewish people by reclaiming their Holy City after more than seventy years. Nothing could stop them from marveling and rejoicing together!

Consider team celebrations in the New Testament. Once Jesus ascended to Heaven, His apostles *"returned to Jerusalem with great joy. And they stayed continually at the temple, praising God"* (Luke 24:52, NIV). Exhilarated by the reality of their Savior's presence, teaching, victory over death, and rising into Heaven, they remained together to rejoice, commune, and pray. Fifty days later, at Pentecost, we find this group still together praying in the upper room, but now with about 120 people. There is power in rejoicing together with Christ being the central focus.

The question, then, is why we are not celebrating His victories here on earth more often.... If sports teams have a temporal, less significant reason to yell, jump, and erupt, don't Christians have an even greater reason to do it? We have good reason to celebrate!

What reasons hold Christians back from jubilation and celebration?

_____

_____

_____

_____

_____

_____

_____

How then can churches celebrate more? First, pastors should demonstrate a sincere spirit of gratitude to God and rejoicing from the platform. People follow those who lead with conviction and boldness. Lead your people to express thankfulness and joyful expression to our Savior. Furthermore, highlight specific "wins" in and through the church body. These unify the team. People see that vision is being implemented and successes realized, and that is exciting. Second, make a big deal of individual efforts and victories. While small progress is often overlooked by many, attentive leaders pay attention and recognize it publicly.

Use a nicely assembled video and photo montage of recent events to convey successes or victories. Set aside time for testimonies of God's work during the church service or small group. I heard it said that giving an old-fashioned witness is the lifeblood of the church. Why? People want to hear good news and see that God still transforms lives. Leaders should build testimonies into their agenda more often than they do, I believe.

Have you considered that communion and baptisms are celebratory? In baptism, we celebrate their commitment to Christ, their salvation, their public declaration that they are on the winning side of eternity, and their step of obedience. Help people to understand the reasons to rejoice in this. Clap your hands and shout for such victories! And when we eat and drink the elements of communion, indeed there is a component of somber reflection at Christ's death, but what else does communion recognize? Jesus said to take the bread and the cup in remembrance of Him, of His perfect redemption, of His unfathomable glory, of His sweet return, of His life within us. I view communion as a reason to rejoice privately and corporately.

Churches are energized by our time of rejoicing as a team—we need that time together. Then the wise leader will redirect the team's focus to the mission still before them. Jesus reminded His disciples that the fields *"are ripe for harvest"* (John 4:35, BSB), helping lift their eyes to the ongoing mission waiting to be fulfilled. Reflect on the past and get ready for what still lies ahead. Times of celebration have a place and purpose, and then we ought to point right back to the mission before us. **Let your rejoicing lead to recommitment!**

Churches that celebrate well . . . live to tell!

GOING DEEPER

1. When was the last time your church intentionally rejoiced together? What was the catalyst?

_____

_____

_____

_____

_____

_____

2. Name some current or upcoming opportunities for your church to rejoice together.

_____

_____

_____

_____

_____

_____

3. How would you rate your own habit of regularly celebrating God and His work in you?

_____

_____

_____

_____

_____

CHAPTER 10

MONUMENTAL INNOVATION: LEADING INTO THE FUTURE

"On that day a great persecution broke out against the church in Jerusalem, and all except the apostles were scattered throughout Judea and Samaria. . . . Those who had been scattered preached the word wherever they went."
—*Acts 8:1, 4 (NIV)*

You have likely evaluated yourself, your ministry, and your future as a leader. Naturally, you've had some successes and a few failures along the way. Let's get one thing clear—leading is difficult and even the best leaders of organizations sometimes stumble in decision-making. Not all of your choices will be the best ones; some will turn out to be adequate; some will be amazing. All leaders should show themselves grace while seeking to learn from earlier choices. In a multitude of counselors, there is wisdom. Pastors, especially, need their boards and a trusted group of advisors to consider various implications of each decision. No one person should attempt grand changes alone.

Name one leadership decision you made that turned out poorly. Then name one decision that made you look like a star.

_____

_____

_____

_____

_____

_____

As we work through the following pages, ask yourself, "What does it take to produce monumental change? Am I ready for what is demanded, and how can I ready myself?" Use this as a time of self-reflection of your own grit. Every season of change requires a leader who decides to take up the mantle to forge a pathway. In fact, a smooth transition of change within an organization requires personal development and preparation of the entire leadership team. Choosing to entertain the possibilities ahead requires courage at this stage. Be encouraged, though. If the Lord has arranged for you to lead at this time in history, accept that you may be the Esther of your day for such a time as this. Where He leads you, His grace will sustain you.

At times, change is forced upon us when we, or our churches, face a fork in the road, a significant decision that must be chosen from among multiple options. Failure to act may result in stagnation and frustration, and even decline. Hard choices must be made, and it will fall on your shoulders to make them.

When has the need to pivot in methods ever forced your hand to make a change?

_____

_____

_____

_____

_____

_____

_____

Consider the national shutdown again in 2020. Did church leaders desire to move their worship services online as their primary means of ministry for several months? No way! But did churches change their methods to accomplish the greater good of ministry, given the circumstances? Absolutely. The ones who refused to change significantly struggled to survive that season. Pivoting, or changing directions, is necessary for not just growth, but survival in some cases. When persecution broke out against the early followers of Christ in Jerusalem after Stephen's martyrdom, everyone scattered, except the apostles (Acts 8:1-4). What the enemy meant for evil, God turned for good. The Gospel spread throughout Judah, Samaria, Galilee, and beyond! Change was forced upon them, and they accepted the need to pivot, which required sacrifice, but also reaped great fruitfulness.

Using new and creative means to achieve the greater ends in ministry—salvation, discipleship, community, and service—is like taking the Gospel from horse-and-buggy to a Tesla.

While unfamiliar at first, innovative change proves to be a worthwhile endeavor for the present and the future. I'd like to expand on four wise principles of leading change: Innovation, Integration, Incubation, and Implementation.

In *Leading the Revolution*, Gary Hamel, one of the world's foremost thinkers on management and business strategy, distinguishes between *innovation* and methodology. One could compare it to the difference between macroevolution (from one species to an entirely new species) and microevolution (adaptations within a species). The introduction of the smartphone was an innovation, as there was a dramatic shift from a device that only made phone calls to one that had Wi-Fi capability, a significant leap in functionality and purpose. That significant move was not a simple upgrade of features, as between one Apple iPhone and the next year's model. These upgrades would simply involve enhancements of existing products and systems. Another innovation that "changed the game" involved the personal transportation industry. Uber broke the mold by using individuals' own cars, GPS tracking, and a revolutionary system. That is innovation! The world will not return to the old system.

What other products, services, or systems would fall under the category of Innovation?

_____

_____

_____

_____

_____

_____

_____

Monumental innovation will lead to significant growth and that can involve new models that transcend present models and systems. What some pastors do is look at what other pastors have done down the road or across the country and attempt to replicate it in their own organizations. Others' packaged ideas, however, may not be right for another geographic region or population. The innovative leader evaluates the core issues facing an industry or field, constructs models of current trends, and makes proactive changes to be at the cusp of those trends.

One prime example of innovation in the world of Christianity involves moving from the printed Bible to a digital page on Bible apps like YouVersion. The pages of the Bible now live on a microchip within your device or in cyberspace and can be accessed instantaneously throughout the world. Accessibility and delivery of the scriptures completely changed with the genesis (no pun intended) of these apps. You and your circle of friends may use it, along with 500 million others. A game changer!

Also in the church world, the use of video messages was innovative in the early 2000's. Craig Groeschel, pastor of Life.Church, a now multi-site, nationwide church network, stumbled upon this idea when preparing to be away one Sunday from his one-site church building. What began as a secondary plan snowballed over time to a new system to show a pre-recorded video at another campus location, which then evolved to live streaming it to multiple locations as Wi-Fi functionality expanded. Innovation occurred because a need, or a crisis, demanded it. As a result, now millions of people are hearing the Gospel and maturing in their faith. This is the power of innovative change from outside-the-box thinking.

The next "I" stands for *integration*. For change to occur in churches, the pastor states the goal, explains why change is needed, and casts a vision to a strategic "change team" of leaders who develops a plan. Leading this core group to believe in and invest in this collective sense of destiny holds enormous weight during this stage, empowering them to dream of unconventional strategies and uncover deep capabilities of the team. Integrating the vision for something grander swells within this smaller group, inspiring these members to become primary catalysts of thought generation and change.

Who would you ask to be a part of your "change team"?

_____

_____

_____

_____

_____

_____

_____

_____

This vision and plan then must move through the whole church body. It is all-hands-on-deck to see this through. Talk about it often. Passing a clear vision and plan to the entire church body acts as yeast in dough, systematically and organically integrating and expanding, creating a richer identity together under a new mission. The key is to build firm trust with the church body at this critical juncture so that they willingly invest their hearts and minds with you in the coming work.

Compare this principle to inviting guests to become more involved in your church—some will run toward that center while others will meander and get there eventually. What conditions facilitate this process? You provide more and more exposure through various means of communication to convey the heart of your church, showing pictures and videos of your church family, the worship experience, serving together, and other events. Churches use Creative Teams, social media, emails, phone calls, texts, and letters to keep the essence of their church in front of them. In the same way, wise leaders will keep the vision of needed change before the body often and through various methods. He or she will speak of it from the platform, in e-communication, with other leaders, in small groups, and on social media. The vision permeates the crowds through regularly seeing it posted and hearing it stated, and it becomes the norm. **To integrate, you must communicate, and do it often.**

Third, change requires a phase of *incubation*. Like sowing seeds into cultivated soil and providing regular nourishment, a vision takes time to root and grow. Change needs to become part of the DNA of a church and that takes time. When leaders let a vision incubate, they give it time to breathe, allowing the whole group to become increasingly accustomed to the idea of something new.

Gradual acceptance can be the key to gaining group support. People should not be rushed to acceptance too quickly. A guiding coalition of team members waters and feeds the vision, vibrantly conveying plans and the changes to come. This phase requires patience in leaders since people embrace change at differing rates. Consider some strategic changes in churches over the years that ruffled many feathers—going from hymns to praise & worship songs, hymnals to screens on the wall, pews to theater seating, choir robes to casual clothes, the pastor's suit and tie to business casual and very casual. Most of us can remember these changes and realize that they took time to incubate . . . a long time. People get used to the familiar, so we must give them freedom to mentally and emotionally transition to new methods that have grown out of an expressed vision. As many moms across the world have said over the years, "You can't rush good cooking." For our discussion, you can't rush new ideas because, when all is said and done, you want people to still be walking with you. Such is wise leadership. Such is the benefit of incubation.

Try to recall the feeling of being rushed into making a change. Was it mostly positive or negative? How would you go about conveying to a group that an impending change is approaching?

_____

_____

_____

_____

_____

_____

_____

_____

_____

The final "I" is *implementation*, which pertains to enacting the components of a change event—the speed of the rollout, the visual progress of new changes, how they are communicated, the frequency of their mentioning, how leaders model change through their attitudes and practice, and handling challenges. Now begins the work of making the change happen. Buildings start to break ground, renovations take place, products are rolled out to the public, sponsorship letters are mailed, and staff members are hired. Action has begun and this is an exciting time!

As you implement, be aware of obvious and subtle obstacles and take steps to remove them. These involve having serious conversations with resistant members to alleviate concerns, helping them see the deeper purposes of change, and encouraging them to support it. It also involves evaluating what is going well and what is not, learning from successes and mistakes, adapting methods without deviating from the vision. Implementation consists of building momentum and excitement through identifying those who have made changes happen along the way, recognizing their individual efforts.

Negativity will undoubtedly arise as the process wears on, which can discourage the team, so celebrate short-term wins often. Prepare weekly updates for everyone to acknowledge victories that were achieved. Every step forward should be tied back to the vision and why you all are walking through a season of forward-thinking change. Keep celebrating until the mission is fulfilled! As I stated in the previous chapter, once you have your final celebration at the culmination of all that work, ready yourselves to get back to work to build the Kingdom.

Preparing for growth takes time, thoughtfulness, and sacrifice from everyone. But for the lead change agent at the helm of the ship, it requires fortitude and courage, especially when asking others to traverse the waters of the great unknown to achieve the greater good. We rely on the stability of our Savior and assurance of His leading to find personal comfort and hope. Such an attitude exemplifies to the entire group how to live graciously through the transitions and sacrifices. All the while, people are watching you, as well as the leadership team, looking for direction, example, and hope that the congregation will survive this season of change.

Perhaps the greatest deficit the church is facing today is a leadership deficit. You are currently in the unique place you sit now because of the providence of God for the purpose of God with the people of God. You are there for such a time as this. Change often begins with just one person who is relentlessly pursuing God and His will. Be that person who listens to God and obeys His leading at the expense of that which is comfortable and normal. Your family, church, community, and untold numbers of people need you to thoughtfully, intentionally, and courageously lead them through the change process.

Monumental innovation involves more than simply changing methods. Ministers and ministries married to their method more than their mission will meet their demise. So, let's get ahead of the curve and allow ourselves and our teams to think deeply and dream richly. Seek the Lord's guidance, along with that of gifted leaders, in your planning. There is wisdom in much counsel. Forge ahead and blaze a trail to fulfill Jesus's Great Commission—*"Go make disciples of all nations...."* For the sake of God's ever-expanding Kingdom, embrace change and boldly follow the mission He has prepared for you ... the mission that leads outside the box!

GOING DEEPER

1. Describe the detrimental effects of speeding through the change process among a large group of team members or a congregation.

_____

_____

_____

_____

_____

_____

_____

_____

2. What current changes do you perceive are needed in your church or organization?

_____

_____

_____

_____

_____

_____

_____

3. Thinking ahead three to five years from now, what challenges might you and your leaders face? How can you begin to pivot now to best prepare for those challenges?

_____

_____

_____

_____

_____

_____

CPSIA information can be obtained
at www.ICGtesting.com
Printed in the USA
BVHW050753110523
663882BV00008B/15